BRISTOL LODEKKAS

STEPHEN DOWLE

AMBERLEY

Acknowledgements

I must record my debt to two websites: Rob Sly's Bristol Commercial Vehicles Enthusiasts (bcv. robsly.com), which undertakes to record the histories of all Lodekkas and the whereabouts of surviving examples; and Bus Lists on the Web (buslistsontheweb.co.uk), an invaluable resource for chassis, body and registration numbers, first owners and dates into service.

Many of the photographs that follow have appeared on Flickr and its members have often contributed extra information concerning the vehicles depicted.

First published 2017

Amberley Publishing
The Hill, Stroud
Gloucestershire, GL5 4EP

www.amberley-books.com

Copyright © Stephen Dowle, 2017

The right of Stephen Dowle to be identified as the Author of this work has been asserted in accordance with the Copyrights, Designs and Patents Act 1988.

ISBN 978 1 4456 6463 7 (print)
ISBN 978 1 4456 6464 4 (ebook)

British Library Cataloguing in Publication Data. A catalogue record for this book is available from the British Library.

Typesetting by Amberley Publishing.
Printed in the UK.

Introduction

The Bristol Lodekka derived from two prototypes constructed by the Bristol Tramways & Carriage Company in 1949. One was placed with the company's own operating fleet and the other with the West Yorkshire Road Car Co. Each was demonstrated to various operators within the nationalised Tilling Group companies. The new vehicle was conceived as the solution to a problem that afflicted almost every bus operator: low railway bridges. The overall height of a double-decker was made up of the clearance between the road and the lower deck floor, plus lower deck headroom, plus upper deck headroom. Around a foot could be saved by resorting to the hated 'lowbridge' or 'skittle-alley' layout, in which the upper deck was provided with four-abreast seats and a sunken gangway at the offside, imperilling the heads of those who were incautious in rising from the seats beneath. Without this layout no double-decker could be constructed to a height less than about 14 feet 5 inches.

The matter really hinged on the irreducibility of the height of the lower deck floor, which had to clear the prop-shaft and differential gear. The Lodekka's innovation lay in a clever redesign of the transmission. The idea evidently didn't spring fully formed into the minds of Bristol's engineers, for the prototypes drove to the rear wheels by way of a splitter box and separate shafts. This arrangement proved unsatisfactory and by 1953, when six pre-production models were built for various Tilling companies, the designers had developed a new layout in which the prop-shaft was displaced to the offside and drove a drop-centre rear axle. This made it possible to eliminate the step from the entrance platform to the lower deck floor and correspondingly reduced the height of the entire vehicle, permitting conventional upper deck seating within lowbridge dimensions.

All Lodekkas were bodied by Eastern Coachworks of Lowestoft. Like Bristol's chassis-building works, the coach works had come to the Tilling Group with the acquisition of its parent company. In 1955 Bristol's Motor Construction Works were separated from the operating company, the two businesses becoming Bristol Commercial Vehicles (BCV) and Bristol Omnibus Co. The Bristol Tramways prototype lasted until April 1963. As a schoolboy living on the edge of the city, my interest in buses must have begun about a year before that. In spite of this overlap I have no recollection of ever seeing it. My early allegiance was to the K-type and its derivative, the KSW. It must be conceded that the new bus was no beauty. The prototypes were provided with massive radiators and, a bizarre addition, a front bumper. The reduced height gave them a notably squat appearance and window spacing produced a fussy quarter-width window ahead of the platform. For the pre-production vehicles the designers had adopted what became known as the 'new look' front, in which the engine, radiator and nearside wing were enclosed within a structure called a cowl. In the first production version, dubbed the LD-type, this was given a subtle re-styling, but the complete vehicle retained a dumpy, rather bulbous look. I thought it a graceless pudding of a thing, my objection being mainly to the cowl. The cab, bonnet, radiator and trembling expanse of mudguard, seen close-up as a KSW drifted to rest at a bus stop, pleased me greatly. In a K-type there was also a quick look at the mysterious autovac pump. These simple enjoyments were lacking from the boxed-in front of an LD.

My low opinion of the Lodekka changed the moment I first clapped eyes on its final form, the FLF-type. Instead of the LD's dim tungsten bulbs, its interior blazed with florescent light. It was longer and more graceful than its predecessor but, more sensational than this, passengers boarded and alighted at a forward entrance with folding doors; I had never before seen a bus with anything but an open platform at the back. The fabulous vehicle growled past in the twilight on the last few yards of its approach to Bristol's bus station; it had been on the service from Bath, an early recipient of the new type. Addicted to timetables, maps and the planning of expeditions, I made preparations for an early visit to Bristol's fabled Georgian neighbour. My mother, however, would allow this only if I took a friend with me. From my classmates at school I selected a rather dim boy, not exactly a friend but a kind of acolyte. Knowing that the outing depended on his participation and not wishing to discourage him, I neglected to mention that its sole purpose was to travel on one of the new buses. At the bus station I let two Bath-bound KSWs depart without us. KSWs were, for the time being, old hat. Notwithstanding my attempts to appease him with Refreshers (it was Saturday, pocket-money day, and I had stocked up on confectionery), the vibes of incomprehension emanating from my companion were palpable. Putting aside my usual preference for the upper deck I insisted, to his further annoyance, on sitting downstairs to observe operation of the folding doors. Back at school, though our relations had been cordial, there was a new coolness in his demeanour.

My schoolboy interest in buses took a back seat to other preoccupations as the years passed. My first job lasted for four years, but the firm then moved to a site some miles outside Bristol and on the opposite side from the easterly suburbs where I lived. Travelling back and forth daily by public transport would be impractical. I needed another job quickly. In that age of full employment, bus operators found it difficult to recruit staff and any applicant was almost guaranteed acceptance. Thus, in April 1970, I became a bus conductor working from Lawrence Hill depot on one of the Bristol 'city' services. At the time, the city fleet consisted of diminishing numbers of my old favourites, the KSWs, working alongside LDs – also becoming fewer – and a full complement of FLFs.

In magazines and elsewhere you sometimes read the reminiscences of former bus drivers concerning particular types, but what about the poor, unregarded bloke on the back, his opinions unsought? As a conductor's bus I thought the LD decidedly inferior to the KSW. I disliked the position of the 'conductor only' bell-push on the platform, behind my head. This meant that I had to turn my hand through 180 degrees, with the palm facing backwards. In the KSW the button had been to one side, about level with my right ear. The KSW's lower deck gangway was level with the bottom step of the stairs. This engendered the habit of stepping directly from one to the other. When going from the lower to the upper deck, with the 'slingshot' effect of a good swing on the stanchion at the bottom of the stairs, one was carried halfway up by pure momentum. In the LD, with its flat floor, one had to step around the bottom step and haul one's self aloft from platform level. These may seem trivial objections, but I often noticed that maintaining energy levels was as much a psychological as a physical matter, and these small things made a difference to one's 'form'. The KSW was also provided with a tiny landing at the top of the stairs, commanding a good view of the platform and an extra bell-push on the back of the rearmost seat. This landing was absent from the LD, although a more-or-less unusable bell-push was retained. The FLF was fine: everything was conveniently positioned for the conductor; he had a 'cubby hole' at the foot of the stairs where he could stand without impeding the ingress and egress of his passengers. The bell-push was out of sight in the luggage pen and came nicely to the right hand. Some thought had gone into what we later came to know as 'ergonomics'.

By the mid-seventies, after a number of false starts, the introduction of driver-only operation was getting into its stride. With its perennial shortage of staff the company was eager to re-train conductors, and complete non-drivers such as myself were not discouraged. This was how I learned to drive, avoiding the fees and the six-month waiting list to which ordinary mortals were subjected in those days. I trained partly on KSWs but mostly on LDs, passing my PSV driving test, very much to my own surprise, on one of the latter during the first days of May 1976. Separate training on FLFs was thought unnecessary, since they were merely a development of the LD; trainees were merely 'familiarised'. In my case familiarisation consisted of two or three circuits of the yard of Lawrence Hill depot. As a novice I found the FLF considerably more of a handful than the LD and the first one I properly drove was the bus in which I set out to pick up my first passengers. 'Thrown in at the deep end' and 'baptism of fire' are phrases that suggest themselves; it took me six months to feel confident.

So what were they like? An early impression was that the driving position was not as good as in the KSW, whose steering-wheel was in an almost horizontal plane. This enabled the driver to get on top and put his shoulders into the steering – an important consideration in those days before power-assistance, when steering had to be low-geared. The Lodekka's wheel was angled backwards and less comfortable. I was also not keen on the obstructed view to the nearside caused by the 'cowl', although I noticed this less with experience. The driver's surroundings were spartan; instrumentation was minimal and controls completely basic. The wiper motor was not always well sealed and in wet weather the resulting drip fell with pinpoint accuracy on one's right knee. The passengers' bell, especially when rung for the same bus stop by several different passengers, or several times by a single passenger who couldn't hear it, could be irritating. The mechanism was usually found to be muted with inserted pieces of fag-packet. In the FLF there were two engine options, the Bristol BVW and the Gardner LW: the latter was, in my opinion, much the better. Whereas the LW did instantly what the right foot requested of it, the BVW always seemed unresponsive and it was difficult to do anything with delicacy. Brute force and ignorance was the only method and one easily became fatigued.

The essential skill for any driver was gear changing. As we were often reminded at the driving school, there was only one way to change gear with a 'crash' gearbox – properly. It was all in the matching of engine revolutions to road speed; a simple enough concept, but a ticklish business in practice. Today I bite my tongue and smile benignly when I hear a motorist claim that 'you can't call yourself a driver if you haven't passed your test in a manual car'. Properly considered all modern cars are automatics, the so-called manual gearbox being in fact a synchromesh, in which the speeds of the rotating shafts are automatically synchronised before coupling, removing all judgement from the operation. It was otherwise in the Lodekka. Even the simple matter of waiting for the revs to drop when changing up was not without its complexities. Especially in the superbly engineered Gardner engine, the wait could be of considerable duration. The usual starting gear was second, first being used only for hill starts. The trouble with trying to get away on even a slight uphill slope was that by the time the revs dropped to the point at which a change could take place, the bus would have stopped and been rolling backwards. This is where the 'snatch' change came in: first gear was used to take up the initial starting effort; then, with the wheels barely turning the driver hit the clutch pedal and executed a lightning 'straight through' change into second. Some gearboxes were more amenable to this technique than others. Changing down was achieved by the double de-clutch method, in which one application of the clutch was used to disengage the higher gear and a second to engage the lower. During the pause in neutral the driver 'gunned' the engine to increase the revs to the speed required in the lower gear. Misjudgement resulted in failure and noisy re-attempts. A missed change at the top of a hill could result in an uncontrolled descent, unrestrained by 'engine braking'. For this reason the Bristol company insisted that buses be stopped at the tops of certain 'compression hills' and descend from rest in second gear. In practice you also tended to use a double action of the clutch on upward changes, for the simple reason that keeping the pedal depressed every time you waited for the revs soon had your left leg complaining. The FLF allegedly was fitted with a device called a clutch brake. A single application of the clutch operated a brake on the engine flywheel, which quickly slowed the revs and made a faster change possible. My impression was that the company regarded it as inessential and didn't bother to maintain it. On the rare occasions when I encountered a working example I was taken by surprise.

Another complication was the famous five-speed gearbox fitted to many Lodekkas. The first four gears were in the conventional 'H' configuration. In fourth the gearstick moved from side to side as though in neutral; fifth was engaged by moving the stick to the right, against your leg, and then forward. This meant that there had to be another neutral position between fourth and fifth, and that once in fifth, no other gear could be engaged without returning through fourth. It was commonly said that if the bus came to rest in fifth, you had to stop the engine in order to get back to second and move off again, but I don't remember encountering this problem. With the side-to-side 'waggle' of the stick in fourth, it almost seemed that the gearbox had three neutral positions. It is said that this bizarre configuration was needed because the fifth gear was simply grafted on to the side of the standard four-speed box. The tale is told of a preservationist who owned an LD for twenty years without ever discovering that it had a fifth gear. Really, the Lodekka was ill-suited to the stop-go urban conditions in Bristol, which must have been the largest city whose bus service was not provided by the municipality. The Bristol company was part of the nationalised group, with a fleet adapted to rural and inter-urban services, typified by long spells of uninterrupted running. A municipal operator would have used a more advanced, labour-saving vehicle.

If the Lodekka had a weakness, it was the heating and cooling system invented by Wing-Commander Cave-Brown-Cave, professor of engineering at Southampton University. A distinctive feature of the vehicle was the pair of shuttered openings on either side of the destination screen, and the first question that came to mind when you opened the bonnet was, 'Where's the radiator?' The Cave-Brown-Cave (CBC) system replaced the radiator with a pair of heat exchangers between the decks which, as well as cooling the engine, so the theory went, could also heat the interior of the bus. In the ceiling of the cab were two 'umbrella handles' which, when pulled (there were two loud thumps) opened the shutters to admit warm air. There were endless problems of overheating. The basic snag, so it was said, was air-locks in the system and also something more fundamental, which was poor air flow caused by the simple fact that a bus is a relatively slow-moving vehicle making frequent stops. Bristol sits in a bowl and from the centre of the city the way lies uphill in all directions. Boil-ups as buses laboured fully laden for the suburbs in slow traffic during the evening peak could be spectacular, with fountains of scalding water and clouds of steam issuing from the breather-hole on the bonnet. With Bristol engines you learned to recognise the hammering sound of an impending engine seizure: Gardners never seized. The company contended with the problem for years. The pipework for the system passed through the cab. Sometimes you clambered into the driving seat and found yourself sitting in the midst of a beautiful contrivance of copper pipes, valves and stop-cocks, which was the company's latest modification to the system. Eventually they seemed to get the problem licked, and in the final years of the FLFs, boilings and engine seizures became a thing of the past. Some operators wouldn't touch the CBC system; those that did tended to drop it from their later orders, and towards the end of production I think it was dropped altogether.

During 1975 I'd begun taking a few photographs of the KSWs, which were down to their last survivors. Finding myself suddenly a driver not long afterwards revived my interest in buses. The LDs were also becoming scarce and it was obvious that once they'd gone the first withdrawals of forward-entrance Lodekkas would follow. Abandoning for once my habitual procrastination I began travelling around to take photographs while there were still substantial numbers to be found. Although I could now drive it was some years before I had a car, and I was restricted to locations that could be reached by train. All buyers of the Lodekka in England and Wales had become subsidiaries of the National Bus Company (NBC), which introduced a particularly feeble corporate livery, soon to be found everywhere from Land's End to Hadrian's Wall. I was too late to record on film the dignified splendour of the old liveries before they were swept away in this tide of mediocrity and standardisation.

In Scotland, however, developments lagged a little behind and when I first went there, on a whistle-stop visit in October 1976, I was delighted to find not just the gloriously old-fashioned liveries of the Scottish Bus Group (SBG) but, in Glasgow, a complementary gloom and decrepitude that reminded me of austerity-era English cities when I was a boy. Let me assure any Scottish reader who may feel affronted that I write these words with approval. For the next few years, a short bus-snapping holiday in Scotland became an annual event.

Scotland had been the setting of a curious episode in the Lodekka's history. The SBG had been an early buyer of the Lodekka's untried successor, the Bristol VRT, which had been built as a longitudinal-engined prototype but then hurried into production in transverse-engined form to comply with a government bus grant specification. Almost immediately cooling and transmission problems were experienced. By the early 1970s the SBG's disillusionment was so complete that it negotiated a deal with the NBC to exchange its entire fleet of VRTs – ninety-one of them by this time – for the same number of FLFs. The NBC fell with alacrity upon this chance to exchange two-man vehicles for newer one-man replacements. The ex-Scottish VRTs went on to serve normal lifetimes in England without exceptional problems. These events brought 'added interest' to the Scottish scene and it was an odd experience for a visiting Sassenach enthusiast to encounter FLFs with the distinctive SBG destination screen groaning through the granite streets in unfamiliar colours, carrying registration numbers issued in Colchester or Reading.

Another sub-plot in the Lodekka story concerned the regulations regarding its sale. As part of the nationalised group, BCV was prohibited, for reasons of governmental logic, from selling its products to customers outside the state-owned sector. To get around this BCV entered into an association with Dennis Motors, licensing that company to manufacture the Lodekka chassis for

Caught during a wardrobe malfunction on a bad hair day, the author poses alongside Alexander Northern No. NRD3 (RVW 394D), newly repainted into the company's unusual yellow and cream livery after transfer from Alexander Midland. Readers will notice that the registration number was issued in Chelmsford: the bus had been new in 1966 to Eastern National and had come to Scotland in exchange for an Alexander Midland Bristol VRT. The photograph was taken at Dundee on Tuesday 26 June 1979.

The Dennis Loline Mk III. Under the Weymann bodywork was a licence-built version of the FLF Lodekka chassis, made for sale to operators such as Aldershot & District, which was part of the British Electric Traction group. The bus reverses from its stand at Guildford bus station on Friday 13 October 1978, by which time the Aldershot company had been merged by the National Bus Company with neighbouring Thames Valley to form Alder Valley.

sale to outside buyers. The Dennis version was called the Loline. The agreement provided for the exchange of technical information between the companies and it was Dennis who developed the epicyclic gearbox which, towards the end of its production life, was made available in the FLF.

In this semi-automatic form the FLF was provided with the 10.45-litre Gardner LX engine. Elongated bodywork, which mostly went to Scotland, was also made available. The FLF had become an impressive machine, made for doing the job. The last examples taken into Eastern National's fleet, in which all these new features were brought together, may be regarded as the final form, not just of the Lodekka, but of the traditional crew-operated, front-engined, half-cab double-decker that had been a feature of the road transport scene, and a uniquely British vehicle recognised the world over, for fifty years. A particular memory, from a few years into my driving days, is of accelerating away from a bus stop outside a house that had become a bed and breakfast hotel. It had a gate set in a tall hedge. As the Gardner engine rasped up to maximum revs, a middle-aged, obviously American couple, for whom the FLF would have been something 'typically British', stepped out onto the pavement, close enough to feel the waste engine heat. They stopped and watched, with unmistakeable looks of admiration.

As we have seen, the Lodekka, on the face of it a highly standardised vehicle, wasn't quite as standardised as all that. It had a story to tell and there had been a few twists and turns in the plot. Was it a successful bus? Over 5,000 were built, a very large total, but it had a captive market. We cannot know whether its buyers would have accepted it if they had not been compelled to. It was a beast, providing little in the way of ease for the men and women who worked on it, or comfort for the passengers who travelled on it. Yet – with a possible reservation concerning the CBC system – it was robust and reliable, qualities guaranteed a warm reception in any company Chief Engineer's office. By the time production of the Lodekka ceased, engineering considerations had become secondary to those of accountancy; the model had been made obsolete by the coming of buses made for driver-only operation which, from an engineering point of view, were far from satisfactory. It is said that Lincolnshire Road Car Co. was getting fuel consumption of 12–13 mpg from its five-cylinder Lodekkas, with engine and gearbox overhauls at around 250,000 miles. With VRTs the figures were around 8 mpg and 90,000 miles. For myself, I can say only that long years of familiarity with the Lodekka – as passenger, conductor and driver – never quite tarnished the lustre it acquired in my eyes when, as a schoolboy, I'd seen my first FLF.

By the mid-1970s the FLF Lodekka was well into the second half of its lifespan, but it was still a familiar sight almost everywhere. With 'maxi' fashions and flared trousers in evidence, Alder Valley's Gardner-engined No. 676 (GRX 144D), followed by a Vauxhall Victor and a Ford Escort van, leaves Reading for Newbury on Wednesday 18 February 1976. The bus had been new to Thames Valley in 1966.

Meanwhile the earliest Lodekka type, the LD, was becoming scarce among NBC subsidiaries. Among the last to retain a substantial fleet was Southern Vectis. Photographed on Monday 15 August 1977 in the parking area of Ryde bus station, the company's No. 558 (PDL 518) was later acquired by Top Deck Travel, an operator of overland tours to the Middle East and Asia. By the 1990s it had returned to Britain and is thought to be in store, pending restoration.

The Scottish Bus Group had the reputation of being conservative in engineering matters. It continued to order the well-tried LD for as long as Bristol Commercial Vehicles was willing to supply it. All vehicles of the final two batches of LDs (Bristol sanction Nos 163 and 177) were supplied to SBG companies and deliveries continued into 1961. No. AA738 in the Eastern Scottish fleet had been new in 1959, but was still clocking up the miles when photographed at St Andrew Square bus station, Edinburgh, on Tuesday 16 May 1978.

The NBC's standard 'leaf green', even when fresh, was not the most beguiling of liveries and always looked dowdy by the time a trip to the paint shop was due. On Friday 3 December 1976 not even the sparkling sunshine of a frosty morning could revitalise the scuffed and unevenly faded paintwork of Bristol Omnibus Co.'s No. 7248 (FHU 506D). The bus was waiting at the unfrequented Southmead terminus of Bristol's cross-city 88 route which, in 1984, became the last in the country to use Lodekkas in all-day service.

One of the less numerous variants of the Lodekka was the FSF-type, which was a 27-foot 6-inch sixty-seater with front entrance. Once the Construction and Use regulations permitted 30-foot double-deckers, the shorter Lodekkas, with their lower seating capacities, rapidly fell out of favour, leaving only the FLF in production. Hants & Dorset had acquired its No. 3477 (VAP 33) from Southdown in 1975, but the vehicle had been new in 1961 to Brighton, Hove & District. It is seen in Blue Boar Row, Salisbury, on Saturday 23 October 1976.

Certain SBG companies modified the fronts of their Lodekkas with circular air intakes for cab heaters, probably of dubious efficiency. In any case Gardner-engined Lodekkas benefited from a 'free' source of heat in that the exhaust manifolds were on the inside, next to the cab, which kept the metal panel next to the driver's leg nicely warmed. Western SMT No. B2427 is seen in Paisley on Monday 25 June 1979. The registration number, issued in Middlesbrough, vouchsafed to the knowledgeable observer that the vehicle had come from United Automobile Services.

During the F-registration year the FLF began to appear with semi-automatic transmission. Such a vehicle was Trent Motor Traction's No. 742 (TRB 570F), which had been new to Midland General and must, at one time, have worn that company's lovely blue livery. Alas, I know it only from photographs. The bus is seen at Nottingham's vanished Mount Street bus station on Saturday 5 May 1979.

An early FLF, from the second (169th) sanction, Cumberland Motor Services No. 509 (510 BRM) was nudging its twentieth birthday when photographed outside the company's Whitehaven garage on Friday 29 June 1979. The adjustable radiator blind and lack of openings on either side of the destination screen tell us that this particular example had no Cave-Brown-Cave apparatus.

During 1962 the Lodekka's bodywork was given a facelift. The radiator grille which, in vehicles with the CBC system, was for appearances only had previously been rather de-emphasised; it was now re-styled and the 'Lodekka' name displayed in the bottom rim. Cream window-sealing rubber replaced black. To my eye the new styling never looked quite right when applied to rear-entrance models: it was all a matter of what you were accustomed to and the origins of my prejudice probably lay in the fact that none of the rear-entrance Lodekkas in my 'home' fleet had the new treatment. Red & White's FS-type No. L5463 (AAX 21B) was snapped at Newport bus station on Friday 20 February 1976.

Baxter's of Airdrie was absorbed by Eastern Scottish in 1962, but its separate identity was perpetuated. Acquisition of the company considerably increased the presence of Edinburgh-based Eastern Scottish to the east of Glasgow. The gorgeous liveries of the SBG companies seemed all the lovelier for the rather cheerless settings in which they were sometimes seen. Blasting its way uphill through the drizzle in Graham Street, Airdrie, on Saturday 7 May 1977, and looking all the more distinguished for its white steering-wheel, was No. AA985 (KPW 486E), which had begun life in England with Eastern Counties.

In 1957 BCV constructed six 'stretched' LDs, designated LDL, to take advantage of new legislation that permitted 30 ft double-deckers. I was too late to get a shot of Bristol's solitary example, No. L8450 (YHT 962), but, on Monday 22 December 1975, tracked it down at Kensington depot, Bath. It had been withdrawn at the end of September and was awaiting disposal. Unfortunately it was parked in an unphotographable position and the best I could manage was this interior shot. Note that the floor under the seats is a little raised above the gangway: this feature was eliminated in the F (for Flat-floor)-series Lodekkas. The 30-foot rear-entrance version that went into production became the FL. The gangway must have passed through the dropped centre of the rear axle, which rises under covers in front of the two inward-facing rear seats.

With a respectable load of homeward-bound shoppers – returning to *Grandstand*, the football results, tea, and *Worzel Gummidge* – Eastern National's No. 2854 (OVX 298D), a Gardner-engined FLF new in 1966, is seen leaving Chelmsford bus station on Saturday 29 March 1980.

A small number of 'time-expired' buses cheated the breaker's oxy-acetylene torch – at least for a while – by being converted for further use in some non-revenue-earning role. Most operators retained the services of a tree-lopping vehicle. Such conversions often resulted from drivers taking unauthorised routes when running empty: even a Lodekka couldn't get under every low bridge. This Gardner-engined LD from 1959 had been new as Midland General's No. 480 (518 JRA). On Saturday 11 September 1976 it carried the Trent fleetname and was photographed at Meadow Road garage, Derby.

Alexander Fife No. FRD 192 (BXA 457B), an FS and, like all Scottish Lodekkas, Gardner-powered, climbs out of Kirkcaldy on Tuesday 16 May 1978. The F-series Lodekkas were the first that had air, rather than vacuum brakes. I had arrived in the town minutes before and the photograph was taken a few yards from the station.

Mansfield District Traction's No. B452 (DAL 307C), new in 1965, was snapped in its home town on Tuesday 16 August 1977. At bottom right we glimpse some detail of NBC uniform. The issue of PSV licence badges was discontinued in 1991. The two letters were a regional prefix: EE was issued by the East Midlands District Traffic Commissioners. The NBC had not yet begun to issue shirts as part of its staff uniform and the driver wears a natty item with a design of hock and Chianti bottles. After I had posted this photograph at a photo-sharing website, he was identified as the late Keith Robinson, a crew driver with Mansfield District. He died young.

I once travelled as a passenger from Liverpool to Warrington on one of Crosville's Gardner LX-engined, semi-automatic FLFs. As a connoisseur of bus acoustics, I wondered whether the LX sounded notably different from the more familiar LW, but came away none the wiser because engine noise was entirely drowned by the cry-baby transmission howl. Crosville's No. DFG 258 (SFM 258F) is seen in the former North Western garage at Macclesfield. North Western's operating area largely disappeared when the Greater Manchester PTE was formed and most of what remained was annexed by Crosville. The bus had probably been 'cascaded' from busy routes on Merseyside to less prestigious duties in this backwater of Crosville's dominions. Note the sophisticated fuelling and watering arrangements.

On Thursday 17 January 1980 the contractors were still applying the finishing touches to Northampton's well-appointed but hideous Greyfriars bus station, which forms the background of this photo. It was demolished in 2014. Dirty, week-old snow lingered in the gutters and the lower panels of United Counties No. 652 (652 EBD), a Bristol-engined FS dating from 1964, are mired with grime from the road. The conductor has understandably closed the folding platform doors. Bringing up the rear are a Fiat 127 and – the 1980s boy-racer's favourite – a Ford Capri.

The FL was never very common. Buyers voted with their orders and once a forward-entrance version became available there was little demand for the rear-entrance thirty-footer. It was found in only a handful of fleets. Lincolnshire Road Car's No. 2701 (OVL 485), dating from 1960, was photographed leaving unlovely Scunthorpe bus station on Monday 9 October 1978 on one of the 'town' services.

At one time the vehicles and liveries of bus operators did much to determine the look of a place, at their best enriching and ennobling their surroundings. Western SMT's rich tawny red was relieved by two cream bands lined out in black and the lettering might have come from the side of an Edwardian tram. In England such things were at an end and the era of garishly mismatched 'Starsky and Hutch' stripes was with us. B1813 (VCS 367) is seen leaving Glasgow's Buchanan bus station on Thursday 18 May 1978, during a period of hire to Central SMT. It was withdrawn later in the year, but went on to see further use with Silver Service of Darley Dale.

The new Buchanan bus station had replaced a congeries of buildings on an adjoining site. I believe the original Buchanan *Street* bus station, seen in the background of this shot and used by Eastern Scottish and Central SMT, was also known as Killermont Street... depending on which company's nomenclature you favoured. Off right of this view was Dundas Street, used by Alexander Midland. I saw them only once: on my next visit, the following spring, they had gone. Central SMT's 1962 FSF6G No. B151 (DGM 451), tungsten bulbs aglow, rumbles over the setts on Monday 18 October 1976.

On Friday 25 January 1980 Plymouth's rebuilt city centre still retained an authentic look of the 1950s, with unaltered shop-fronts and original lettering. Such surroundings suited the Lodekka, which was developed in the post-war years. Western National's Gardner-powered No. 2107 (EDV 519D) had been new in 1966. Western National was one of those companies that favoured the side-by-side destination screen, rather than the T-box.

Cost-conscious operators such as Eastern Counties and Lincolnshire Road Car, blessed with virtually hill-free territories, specified the economical five-cylinder version of the Gardner LW engine. The option was not available in the FLF, which hardly seemed over-powered with a six-cylinder engine. Visits to such places as Cambridge brought frequent 'flashbacks', for the distinctive chugging of the 5LW reminded me of the Bristol L5Gs of my boyhood. Eastern Counties No. LFS 55 (55 CPW) waits outside the station on Thursday 11 August 1977. It must have been a warm day, for the driver has deployed the hinged windscreen. Note the superior non-standard seating.

Building contractors often maintained fleets of staff buses for transporting workers to remote sites, but universal car ownership put an end to the practice. With its cab windows and even headlights painted out, the staff bus career of the former Western National No. 1892 (TUO 486), a Bristol-engined LD new in 1955, is clearly over. It is seen at Frenchay, just outside Bristol, on Tuesday 30 December 1975, during construction of a new housing development.

Another of the splendid liveries of the Scottish Bus Group was the nicely lined-out blue of Alexander Midland. The six-sided destination screen always added a touch of distinction to Scottish Lodekkas, although it was perhaps not so legible from a distance as a conventional display. No. MRD 206 (SVX 279D) had come from Eastern National. On Monday 15 May 1978 it had been abandoned in North Hanover Street, Glasgow, and, from the skid-marks behind its rear nearside wheels, appears to have been immobilised by a brake defect.

Driver's-eye view of an FLF cab. The bus, Bristol Omnibus Co. No. 7087 (530 OHU), had been converted for driver training and the back of the cab had been removed. Apart from the speedometer, the only dial was the air gauge, showing brake pressure front and rear. The Simms box on the right features the electrical 'on-off' switch and push-button starter, as well as the switches for the exterior lights. Just behind is the self-cancelling indicator switch, never a favourite feature of mine. Left of the driving seat are the door open and close buttons with reset and locking switch. Taken Monday 8 October 1979.

The cab of a semi-automatic FLF, Eastern National's No. 2919 (AEV 813F), photographed on Saturday 29 March 1980. No clutch pedal, obviously, and the gearstick pedestal is blanked off with a metal plate. On the steering column is the SCG (Self-Changing Gears) assembly, with its miniature gearstick and gate, mimicking the H-configuration of a conventional shift. Semi-auto must have been a godsend on a few services such as Eastern National's Wood Green–Southend route, but was largely wasted on the FLF, which was used mostly on inter-urban routes involving comparatively little use of the gears.

The former Wilts & Dorset No. 670 (479 BMR) had become Hants & Dorset No. 127 following the merger of the two companies under NBC auspices. The Bristol-engined FS draws alongside a six-month-old VRT in New Canal, Salisbury, on Friday 23 January 1976. Tina gets ready to bail out, leaving Kev to park the Mini. He'll catch her up later in DER, where they can arrange to rent one of the new Betamax videos for their £15,000 semi in Fordingbridge.

Mansfield District Traction's buses seldom carried advertising. This was a matter of policy with certain high-minded operators such as Birmingham Corporation, but doesn't seem to have been a cut-and-dried rule at Mansfield. The company's vehicles always looked notably smart for the lack of garish posters and other disfigurements. The informative three-piece destination display augmented, rather than diminished, the tidy appearance. No. 357 (376 RNN) was new in 1964 and is seen in Mansfield on Saturday 5 May 1979.

Still going strong at eighteen years old on one of its operator's trunk routes was Alder Valley No. 575 (14 DRB), a much-owned, Gardner-engined LD supplied new in 1958 to Notts & Derby. The latter had become a subsidiary of Midland General (itself to be absorbed by Trent Motor Traction in 1976), which passed the vehicle to Thames Valley in 1971. It was photographed at Maidenhead on Wednesday 18 February 1976. An unusual keepsake of its original owner was the four-leaf folding doors – once electrically operated, but now opened and closed by the conductor.

The English FLFs that were exchanged for Scottish VRTs sometimes, but not always, had their original destination screens replaced by the pleasing SBG six-sided type. The same was true, *vice-versa*, of Scottish VRTs in England. Here we see a half-and-half affair in which the original T-box display has been masked by an inverted Scottish screen. Western SMT's No. B2439 (PBL 58F) had come from the Alder Valley fleet. It is pictured at Glasgow's Anderston Cross bus station on Saturday 7 May 1977. Note, top left, the first poster in the iconic 'refreshes the parts other beers cannot reach' campaign.

The first style of Lodekka front grille was carried over from the LD to early examples of the FS. In cases of confusion a useful identifier was that the FS had only a single foot-step next to the number plate, whereas the LD had a symmetrical pair. Crosville's No. DFG 31 (312 PFM) stands at Arpley bus station, Warrington, on Saturday 18 March 1978 next to another bus from the same batch.

Bristol Omnibus Co. showed little interest in the FS: indeed, from the beginning it seemed reluctant to accept the Lodekka, continuing to order the old-fashioned Bristol KSW alongside its early intake of LDs. The company's largest batch of FSs were its convertible open-toppers for the seafront service at Weston-super-Mare. The first of them, No. 8576 (866 NHT), is seen on Friday 7 November 1975, with roof fitted for the coming winter. Now that we're all used to thinking in terms of 'Health and Safety', the open rear platform does look rather dangerous. They didn't seem so at the time and I never heard of anyone falling from one.

With the screen already 'dressed' for its next outward journey, Eastern Scottish No. AA891 (YWS 891) turns into Elder Street, Edinburgh – the approach to St Andrew Cross bus station. The savvy driver changed his destination display while setting down passengers at one of the final incoming stops. This saved vital seconds and meant extra time in the canteen. The bus was a veteran of the Baxter's sub-fleet. Tramlines and electrical 'overhead' now fill this view of stately York Place.

The Lodekka's 1962 facelift anticipated the introduction, due the following year, of registration numbers with year suffix letters. The number now appeared in a 'letterbox' opening incorporating the foot step. Few licensing authorities issued A-suffixes and no Lodekkas carried them. Red & White's Bristol-engined FS, No. L5563 (AAX 24B), was photographed on Wednesday 2 March 1977 negotiating the gateway in Chepstow's fortified wall. Headroom is given as 10 feet 6 inches! After being withdrawn early the following year, the bus passed through the hands of several owners and was exported to Germany in about 1984. After disappearing from view for thirty years it resurfaced recently in Switzerland.

Descending Douglas Street, Dunfermline, was Alexander Fife No. FRD 202 (HXA 402E), a 31-foot FLF from among the final batch of Lodekkas built new for service in Scotland. On Tuesday 26 June 1979, such streets were still lined with varied shops; out-of-town malls had not yet established themselves, online shopping was unheard-of and the march of the estate agents and tattoo parlours had not yet begun.

South Wales Transport was not a natural buyer of Bristol types, but this FSF Lodekka had come from United Welsh when that company was absorbed during the 'rationalisation' programme of the NBC's early years. It had been new in 1961 and, when photographed in Swansea on New Year's Eve 1976, was close to the end of its service lifetime.

As a refugee from the NBC's standardised liveries I had, for several years, taken a short holiday in Scotland. On the 1979 trip I found, to my displeasure, that 'corporate identity' had finally caught up with the SBG. A new 'logo', featuring a stylised saltire and common to all subsidiaries, had replaced the various company fleetnames. It was another triumph of appearances over substance. The Lodekka, perhaps, owed more to substance than appearance. This 1962 example, No. AA874 (YWS 874), was seen on Thursday 28 June standing in what had once been Glasgow's Dundas Street bus station, but had become a mere overspill parking area.

Those few LDs that, for a while, dodged the breaker's yard were sighted in a variety of further employments. The former Western SMT No. B1633 (RAG 399), dating from 1961, was snapped on Durdham Down, Bristol, on Wednesday 5 April 1978, as part of the entourage of Gerry Cottle's Circus. Note the three-piece front cowl.

United Autos lost most, if not all of its Gardner-engined FLFs to the Scottish Bus Group, leaving a Bristol BVW-powered fleet. Its No. 544 (NHN 544E) was such a vehicle, seen on Wednesday 27 June 1979 standing in Middlesbrough's partially reconstructed bus station.

The complex interlocking and overlapping bus operations of the East Midlands were early candidates for rationalisation under the NBC. Midland General No. 705 (BRB 493B) had been supplied new to Notts & Derby in 1964. The Midland General company had been founded to provide motor-bus feeder services to the company's trams. In an example of the tail wagging the dog, Notts & Derby was absorbed by its own subsidiary at the beginning of 1972. In 1977 Midland General was itself absorbed by Trent Motor Traction. The company fleetname would not long survive the date of this photograph, taken outside Derby bus station on Saturday 11 September 1976.

Towards the end of production the FLF was made available with bodywork extended to a little over 31 feet. There was no modification to the chassis. Most of these vehicles went to SBG companies and are sometimes known as the 'Scottish long' FLF. They were identifiable by the near-square dimensions of the rearmost window. Seating capacity was increased, in this case to seventy-six, and luggage accommodation was enlarged. It was an imposing vehicle that meant business. Alexander Fife No. FRD 214 (HXA 414E), dating from 1967, is seen at its stance – to use the Scottish term – at Dundee's bus station on Tuesday 16 May 1978.

Eastern National was, I think, the only English user of the long FLF. The company spoiled its drivers with semi-automatic transmission, which was never used in Scottish Lodekkas. Many of these buses entered traffic on the exacting group of services between Southend and Wood Green. For the driver and conductress of No. 2924 (AEV 818F) on Wednesday 11 October 1978, the overlay at Romford was the opportunity for a sit-down, a chat and a smoke.

A pair of Bristol-engined FS Lodekkas seen outside York station on Wednesday 20 October 1976. The local services were operated under the terms of a joint agreement between West Yorkshire Road Car Co. and York's city council. The buses carried YORK WEST YORKSHIRE as a fleetname. Rear-entrance Lodekkas with these 'droopy' back windows, in which the outer corners were curved at the top, were always of the FS type. Some early examples had the curved inner corners of the LD, but no LD had the curved outer corners. This little wrinkle was surprisingly handy when it came to identifying buses receding into the distance.

Newly out of the paint shop by the look of it and clearly being made ready for a second career, the former Alexander Fife No. FRD 168 (3654 FG), an FS dating from 1963, was looking very spruce when snapped at the company's Kirkcaldy garage on Tuesday 26 June 1979. In fact the bus was to become a driver trainer for the neighbouring Dundee municipal operation, known by this time as Tayside Regional Transport. The trade plate appears to be Tayside's, so I may have captured the actual moment of handover.

It is thought that all Cumberland Motor Services FLFs were fitted with Gardner LX engines, presumably thought necessary because of the company's hilly territory. Super-powered No. 528 (CRM 472C) is seen standing in Whitehaven's 1930s bus station on Friday 29 June 1979. At the time of writing the building was being gutted for apartments behind the façade. The Cumberland garage across the road is to become a hotel.

The chassis-cleaning facilities at Red & White's Tredegar garage, pictured on Friday 20 February 1976. Red & White operated no forward-entrance Lodekkas and No. L1060 (10 AAX) was of the uncommon 30 ft rear-entrance FL type. Although new in 1960, the bus still had four years' work ahead of it and went on to serve a driver-training school.

Closely followed by an East Midland Leyland National, Mansfield District Traction No. 356 (375 RNN) is seen on Saturday 5 May 1979 at Mansfield's bus station. The lack of advertising and the agreeable three-piece destination screen would be enough to distinguish this as a Mansfield vehicle, even if other distinguishing marks were removed. East Midland and Mansfield District had been under the same management since 1972. There were many changes of fleetname and company title but eventually, after deregulation, the two companies became a single entity.

Swinging out into Parliamentary Road from Glasgow's Buchanan bus station on Tuesday 16 May 1978 was Alexander Midland's 1963 FLF No. MRD 184 (VWG 364). It was around 7.30 a.m. and the bus is poorly patronised on this outgoing journey. The streets, still quiet and empty, shimmer in the spring sunshine.

A Lodekka line-up at Bristol's Lawrence Hill depot on Tuesday 18 November 1975. The FLFs have a squarer, more upright front than the more contoured LD on the right. It could be that this was necessary to provide space for seating ahead of the FLF's forward staircase; if so it was a happy accident, for it gave the FLF a more purposeful, business-like appearance. Notice too the deeper wings of the updated front. These led to problems with overheating of the front brakes. Small vertical slots were introduced to direct a flow of air over the insides of the wheels; it was said that this modification was suggested by the Bristol company. From left to right the buses were powered by a Gardner LW, Bristol BVW and Bristol AVW engine, the latter being the last in use in the Bristol fleet.

White steering wheels first appeared on Bristol buses when regulations allowed them to be built to a width of eight feet; they were intended as a reminder to the driver that this was one of the wider vehicles. As we can see in this view, the Lodekka's steering column sloped back at an angle. Sometimes the column seemed shorter or the seat a little higher than usual. This was borderline dangerous, as it was difficult to quickly transfer your foot from the accelerator to the brake pedal without striking the underside of the wheel with your knee. Displaying the lazy man's 'Service' destination, Western National's No. 1942 (VDV 759) was photographed, in its eighteenth year, in Taunton on Thursday 19 February 1976.

Perhaps this view exaggerates the effect, but in the 'Scottish long' FLF almost a third of the vehicle's length appears to overhang the rear axle. The driver would need to take more than usual care, when cornering, of rear-end 'out-swing'. BL 316 (FGM 316D) is seen waiting at the lights outside the Buchanan bus station, Glasgow, on Saturday 7 May 1977.

The former Bristol Omnibus Co. No. LC8440 (YHT 933), a Bristol-engined LD of 1957, was withdrawn in November 1975 and passed to Top Deck Travel, the well-known operator of overland tours. On Sunday 3 September 1978 it was found in the shadow of the Westway elevated road in west London outside the premises of the dealer Omnibus Promotions, one of whose guard dogs observes the photographer with indifference.

The very first FLF Lodekka, Bristol's No. C7000 (995 EHW) was completed by ECW in October 1959. It was then demonstrated to Walter Alexander and Crosville Motor Services before being returned to ECW for its sliding door to be replaced by the four-leaf folding type that became standard. Its introduction in Bristol was delayed by a dispute with the men's union concerning standing passengers. The photograph was taken at Lawrence Hill depot, Bristol, on Thursday 4 March 1976, five months before the bus was withdrawn. It is believed to survive in Hawaii.

Eastern Scottish No. AA223 (CSG 223D) awaits custom at St Andrew Square bus station, Edinburgh, on Thursday 28 June 1979. In a pattern that had become familiar throughout the country, Edinburgh's bus station was accommodated, more or less on sufferance, in the ground floor of an office development and shopping centre; or, alternatively, Scottish Omnibuses (the parent company of Eastern Scottish) had enriched itself by turning the fresh air above its property into revenue-generating floor space.

Quite a few 'time-expired' Lodekkas found themselves pressed into further service during the 1970s 'playbus' fad. One such was the former Eastern Counties No. LKD 176 (UNG 176), an LD new in 1956 and, with its five-cylinder Gardner LW engine, made for these flat easterly regions. It was photographed on Saturday 20 May 1978 in Cambridge's Cattle Market car park. It is thought to have been owned by Cambridgeshire County Council.

In 1967, some years after BCV had discontinued the model, Western National wished to place an order for FSF Lodekkas. Bristol Omnibus Co. was prevailed upon to part with twenty of its Gardner-engined examples. By Monday 24 January 1977, No. 1012 (707 JHY) was wearing NBC poppy red in the Devon General fleet. It is seen reversing from the platform of Exeter bus station. The conductor should have been keeping a lookout at the rear of the lower deck, poised to give bell signals, but what could you expect from the sort of cowboy who wore his satchel around his waist?

The upper deck interior of an Alder Valley FLF with coach seating. The photograph was taken on Monday 29 March 1976, when the vehicle was parked in Alder Valley's Reading garage. It went on to be used as a driver trainer, retaining coach seats to the end.

Another upper deck interior, this time of an Eastern National example with forward-ascending staircase. These were, I think, found only on the late 31-foot FLFs and were rare outside Scotland. Note the cigarette stubbers on the backs of the seats and the practice, once widespread, of slipping Setright tickets under the rim of the seat ahead. The bus was standing in the forecourt of Eastern National's garage and bus station at Wood Green, about to depart for Southend.

By now it was only in Scotland that these gorgeous deep reds with gilt lettering and cream relief were to be found among major companies. The fleet number is prominently carried on a metal plate at the front, greatly preferable to the transfers or tatty stick-on vinyl 'numerals' that had become widespread elsewhere. Central SMT's No. B191 (AGM 691B) was parked in readiness at Glasgow's Anderston Cross bus station on Monday 18 October 1976.

Getting in lane in Blue Boar Row, Salisbury, on Friday 23 January 1976, Hants & Dorset's No. 3478 (WNJ 36) rubs shoulders with a recently delivered Bristol VRT and a Saab V4. The bus, a Bristol-engined FSF dating from 1962, had been new to Brighton, Hove & District and had been absorbed, with the rest of that company's undertaking, by Southdown. The registration keeps alive the original BH&D fleet number.

Outside Cambridge station Lodekkas of the Eastern Counties fleet, jostling for position on the city's local services, were joined by similar vehicles operated by United Counties on routes from further afield. On the afternoon of Saturday 20 May 1978 Bristol-engined FS No. 676 (DNV 676C) leaves for Bedford, while a kindred five-cylinder Gardner-engined vehicle waits across the road in the turning circle.

A bizarre feature of the Eastern Scottish fleet by the late 1970s was these artless homemade radiator grilles. They were not uncommon, though few had been subjected to this degree of butchery. Such oddities 'added interest' to omnibological studies. AA975 (KVF 476E) had come from the Eastern Counties fleet during the FLF-VRT exchanges of the early seventies. The vehicle, with its unlovely SBG corporate fleetname, is seen in Glasgow on Monday 25 June 1979.

So familiar has his posture become that the reader might unthinkingly assume that the driver was eyes-down sending a Tweet; but this was Tuesday 16 August 1977 and mobile phones belonged to the remote future. Our man was probably consulting the duty schedule to check his departure time. Mansfield District No. B485 (SRB 61F), seen in Mansfield, was a Gardner-powered FLF dating from 1967.

As, during the second half of the 1970s, the major operators began to withdraw their oldest FLFs, so this rugged, well-tried workhorse was snapped up by subsequent owners in the independent sector. Edwards, of Joy's Green, near Lydney in the Forest of Dean, acquired this ex-Bristol Omnibus Co. trio through the dealer Omnibus Promotions in December 1977. Gardner engines were generally preferred, the supply of Bristol engine spares having become uncertain; nonetheless, two of these three buses, seen on Saturday 17 November 1979, were Bristol BVW-powered.

Which was the last Lodekka built is a moot point. Only five entered service late enough to be registered in the G-suffix year; three went to Eastern National and two to Midland General. If chassis numbers are our guide then the honours go to Eastern National, but Midland General's pair had later body numbers, suggesting that they were the last completed. They are also said to have been placed in service later. The matter therefore remains contentious. Eastern National's No. 2945 (AVX 974G) was the middle member of the company's threesome. It was a 31-footer and, when new, carried coach seating. The photo was taken at Basildon garage on the afternoon of Wednesday 4 July 1979.

The driver of Southern Vectis No. 606 (BDL 582B) pauses in the act of reversing from the platform of Ryde bus station for an exchange of repartee with a colleague. The bus, an FLF6G new in 1964, is seen on Monday 15 August 1977. It continued to serve the company and the Isle of Wight for a further five years and was afterwards exported. It was last reported in Hawaii and had been fitted with offside folding doors.

It couldn't be anywhere but Edinburgh. Here in former times, it is said, railway smoke rose from Waverley station and hung in the air, trapped in this ravine of granite. Eastern Scottish LD No. AA757 (USC 757) is seen as a training bus on Waverley Bridge on the morning of Monday 18 October 1976. Permanent training buses were usually modified internally, in case the need should unfortunately arise for the instructor to make a dive for the handbrake. For the removal of its L-plate and the fitting of a destination blind, this bus looks as though it could be returned to revenue-earning service in ten minutes.

Crosville's DFG 62 (872 VFM), a Gardner-powered FSF, is pictured leaving the Pier Head, Liverpool, on Monday 16 February 1976. This open, well-lighted terminus might have been made with the visiting lensman in mind. On the left another FSF and a semi-automatic FLF await their next turns of duty. Around the country, one saw the vents on either side of the destination screen modified in various ways as different companies, in their different ways, grappled with the problem of the CBC heating.

BCV's first batch of forward-entrance Lodekkas, the 156th sanction, was composed partly of FSFs and partly of FLFs. This was the first chassis of the first all-FLF sanction, the 169th. It was retained, unfinished and unregistered, as a 'development' vehicle for the testing of modifications and improvements. In 1967, with production being run down and no further developments expected, it was finished and released for sale. It passed to Eastern Counties as No. FLF 348 (LAH 448E). By the time of the photograph, taken in Norwich on Friday 11 June 1976, it had been renumbered FLF 429 and been re-engined from Bristol to Gardner. It eventually passed to Top Deck Travel and is thought to have been scrapped in 1992.

Blasting through Paisley in the middle lane on the morning of Wednesday 17 May 1978 we see Western SMT No. B2426 (SHN 256F), which had come from the Northern General fleet. It had been supplied new to United Autos in 1968. Photographs from the English phase of the vehicle's life show the familiar CBC grilles on either side of the destination screen, suggesting that the system was removed for service in Scotland.

A former Hants & Dorset LD, No. 1368 (SRU 981), seen on Thursday 23 October 1978 during the early days of the National Exhibition Centre. It was the time of that year's Motor Show and the bus, converted to use as a hospitality vehicle, stands at the periphery of the vast, still unsurfaced acreage of car parking. It had been new in 1956 and, in 1961, had its original Bristol engine replaced by a Gardner that had been removed from a Bristol L-type. It retains its trademark Hants & Dorset sun visor. The bus later passed through the hands of several preservationists and is thought to be still active in the Netherlands.

The only 'maintenance' duty expected of a driver was to keep the cooling system topped up. This was an important consideration with Lodekkas, especially those equipped with the CBC system, which could sometimes suffer spectacular losses of boiling water. The driver of Alexander Fife's No. FRD 217 (HXA 417E) conscientiously replenishes his vehicle from a hosepipe at Dunfermline bus station on Tuesday 26 June 1979.

The rounded outlines of the Lodekka, belonging to an earlier phase of design, contrast with the inflexible linearity of Scunthorpe's bus station, whose panels of ribbed cladding had scarcely been conceived to lift the spirits of the notoriously dull steel town's waiting passengers. Lincolnshire Road Car Co.'s No. 2519 (AFE 90B), a five-cylinder FS, had been new in 1964. This early front cowl was plainly not original and had probably been fitted during an accident repair. Fred Trueman advertises a popular libation brewed in Halifax. The photograph dates from Monday 9 October 1978.

Buses typically see twelve to fifteen years' service. By the middle of the 1970s, the oldest front-entrance Lodekkas were becoming due for withdrawal. Disposal to dealers was usually followed by scrapping but a minority saw further use. The dealer British Double Decker set up in the yard of the former Charfield station in Gloucestershire and specialised in refurbishing buses for sale to continental buyers through the port of Harwich. Originally Bristol-powered, but here without an engine, the former Crosville No. DFB 51 (264 SFM) was pictured on Saturday 7 April 1979. It went to Sweden but eventually found its way to Denver, Colorado (probably as a 'genuine London bus'), where it is believed to have been scrapped in 2014.

Spring arrives at Kirkcaldy bus station and, on Tuesday 16 May 1978, Alexander Fife's FS No. FRD 184 (3670 FG) stands in the sunshine awaiting its next trip. One hears again the tick of expanding roof panels and, in imagination, draws a deep draught of the delectable interior aroma, resurrecting from sun-warmed rexine and moquette, the umbrellas, raincoats and summer frocks of a dozen past seasons.

Western National's Gardner-engined No. 2071 (AUO 518B) loads up in Royal Parade, Plymouth, on Friday 25 January 1980. As we can see in the leading lower deck window, some operators specified additional luggage space alongside the staircase, reducing seating capacity of the FLF to sixty-eight.

Let us pause for a look at the Dennis Loline, the licence-built version of the Lodekka. The Loline Mk III was the Dennis-made version of the FLF. This one had been new as North Western Road Car's No. 882 (RDB 882). The Alexander body, with its subtly rounded roofline and sawn-off mudguards, combined with a no-nonsense, almost military indifference to fancy appearances, makes this an impressive vehicle. When seen in this lucky shot, taken as I stepped out of Cheltenham Spa station on Friday 16 December 1977, the bus belonged to Castleways of Winchcombe.

Like neighbouring Aldershot & District, the largest single buyer of the Dennis Loline, Reading Corporation probably felt a duty to support a local manufacturer. Dennis were based at Guildford. Reading's No. 177 (GRD 577D), new in 1966, was another Loline Mk III, but with bodywork by East Lancs. It is seen in Reading on Wednesday 18 February 1976.

Ten years old when snapped at Fareham bus station on Monday 15 August 1977, Hants & Dorset No. 1268 (LEL 655F) was built with a Bristol BVW engine and, I think, semi-automatic transmission – if so, an unusual combination. The coloured dots used to denote a vehicle's home garage were an agreeable little distinction of Hants & Dorset, but why not simply print the name?

In 1977 Eastern Scottish suffered a shortage of serviceable vehicles. To alleviate the problem it acquired a batch of Leyland Titan PD2s from Lothian Regional Transport (the Edinburgh municipal operation) and six of Central SMT's substantial fleet of FSF Lodekkas. These had been the only FSFs to see service in Scotland. The company followed its practice of matching fleet numbers to registrations and No. AA441 (DGM 441) is seen parked in Edinburgh's bus station on Tuesday 16 May 1978. Note the unusual three-piece front cowl. Eastern Scottish withdrew all the FSFs in 1979.

In 1964 British Leyland acquired a shareholding in BCV and Leyland's 0.600 engine became available to the FLF Lodekka. There were few takers. It was the kiss of death; Leyland began a tip-toe process of eliminating competitors to clear the market for its own products and BCV was eventually closed some twenty years later. The first three FLF6Ls went to Bristol Omnibus Company. Here, on Wednesday 24 May 1978, the middle member of the trio, No. C7130 (823 SHW), is seen in Church Road, Filton. The bus had been withdrawn, but a vehicle shortage had forced a hurried reinstatement, which accounts for the lack of a fleetname, advertising or fleet number plate. The 'puncture repair' in the roof dome, where there had been an aerial, suggests that radio equipment had been salvaged. The bus went on to serve another year.

With their body panels creaking and clicking in the sunshine, a line-up of Eastern Counties FS-types stands at Cambridge on Saturday 20 May 1978. The cab-side windows of the Lodekka's bodywork underwent subtle re-styling over the years. Originally the bottom edges of the two windows, and the beading underneath, were curved in a 'flow line' above the wheel; there was a 'transitional' phase in which the beading was straight but the bottoms of the windows remained curved. Finally, beading and window-bottoms became straight, as we see here.

The LD at the head of this Lodekka parade, seen on Thursday 28 June 1979, outside the Eastern Scottish Bathgate garage, had been new in 1961. In England the model had essentially been curtailed in 1959, although deliveries continued into 1960. This meant that the LD survived well into the early 1980s in Scotland, some years after its extinction south of the Tweed.

A queue forms in the upper deck gangway as passengers wait to file down the stairs of Southern Vectis No. 570 (YDL 315), which had arrived only seconds before the photograph was taken. The cab is unoccupied however, and the driver and conductor must have already been en route for the canteen, there to assuage the busman's well-known thirst for tea. The Gardner-engined FS was withdrawn in 1980 and sold directly to a preservationist. It remains active on the rally circuit. The photo was taken at Newport bus station on Monday 15 August 1977.

Dating from 1961, Crosville FSF No. DFG 59 (869 VFM) stands in what had once been the forecourt of Arpley station, Warrington, but had become, by Monday 16 February 1976, the town's bus station. The sagging corrugated iron shelters, rutted apron, and the view through iron railings of melancholy dripping twigs and pigeon-haunted paths, engendered a certain ennui; but the services of several diverse operators converged here, and for the enthusiast it was a place of lively interest.

Where but in Scotland? Three Lodekkas in three different liveries go their separate ways as they leave Glasgow's Buchanan bus station on the morning of Thursday 18 May 1978. Alexander Midland's FLF No. MRD 188 (AMS 6B) turns north on one of the services along the Kirkintilloch corridor; Eastern Scottish LD No. AA853 (WSC 853) carries an inward-bound destination and was probably returning to its garage at the end of the morning peak; bringing up the rear is Central SMT No. BE270 (CGM 970C), bound for one of the Lanarkshire suburbs.

As FLFs were withdrawn, small numbers were retained for conversion to driver training vehicles. It was a familiar pattern. The former Bristol Omnibus Co. No. C7200 (CHY 418C) is seen at the company's Lawrence Hill depot on Saturday 8 December 1979 alongside an elderly KSW trainer. The Bristol company had fitted radiators with pressure caps to its remaining FLFs. Water under pressure can be raised to a higher temperature without boiling.

Bristol-engined No. 2100 (EDV 512D) in the Western National fleet is pictured crossing the River Tone, which gives its name to Taunton, on Thursday 19 February 1976. The company was one of those that specified an outside mechanism for changing the destination display, which thereby became the conductor's responsibility. Others favoured an apparatus inside the cab. The area for the destination screen could accommodate a 'T-box' or three-piece display; this side-by-side configuration made rather uneconomical use of the space. Appearances were not helped by the untidy masking of the screen to show only a single line of the blind. Blinds were inclined to slippage, resulting in the unfortunate half-and-half effect seen here.

To the trained observer it was all in the registration marque, issued at Chelmsford: Alexander Midland's No. MRD 200 (RWC 942D) had started life with Eastern National. The SBG had, not unreasonably, insisted on the newest, manual gearbox, Gardner-engined FLFs in exchange for its newer VRTs; this D-registration example must have been among the older vehicles involved in the exchange. It is pictured in Kyle Street, Glasgow, a minute or two after leaving the Buchanan bus station, on Thursday 18 May 1978.

Hants & Dorset No. 1128 (4386 LJ) seen leaving West Marlands bus station, Southampton, on Monday 15 August 1977. Note the hopper vents of the front upstairs windows and the non-standard radiator grille. The bus, an FS6G, passed to Western National for conversion to a driver trainer and afterwards travelled overland to the Middle East and India. It was subsequently reported from Australia, New Zealand, Chile, Mexico and Canada, and returned to Britain in 2008. It is believed to be still active on the continent.

Seen against a fabulous period Glasgowscape, one of the numerous 1961 deliveries of Eastern Scottish LDs, No. AA856 (WSC 856), sets out on Thursday 28 June 1979. The bus appears to belong to Bathgate garage, at the midway point of the long route to Edinburgh.

Bags of omnibological interest at Newport's open and photographer-friendly bus station on Friday 25 March 1977. One of the municipality's Metro-Scanias roars past, but all the other vehicles we see are from National Bus Company fleets, including a Leyland National in the unique NBC blue of Jones of Aberbeeg. Red & White's L6762 (1 EWO) was a Gardner-engined FS new in 1962, and originally numbered L162. It would be surprising if its highly covetable registration number had not been appropriated for further use.

A pair of Mansfield District FLFs, Nos 455 (FNN 157D) and 488 (SRB 64F), pictured at Mansfield's bus station on Saturday 5 May 1979. The relief band beneath the upper deck windows was painted out in the standard NBC liveries and, in any case, ECW had ceased to provide for it by the time these buses were constructed.

Alexander Fife's No. FRD 156 (YWS 871) had started life in 1962 in the Eastern Scottish fleet. The Fife company had acquired it in February 1974 to replace, and assume the identity of, an FLF (7404 SP) that had overturned and been scrapped. The number must have carried a curse, for this second FRD 156 was withdrawn after crashing into a shop window. The photograph was taken on Tuesday 16 May 1978 at Kirkcaldy bus station.

Auld Reekie's own. Eastern Scottish No. AA44 (CSG 44C), based at nearby New Street garage, is seen standing in the parking area of Edinburgh's bus station on Tuesday 16 May 1978. The frontal appearance is slightly unconventional: the CBC vents are of the type normally used at the side and, although the rim of the radiator grille is of the normal type, its mesh is not. The cowl incorporates no foot-step, although there appears to be a grab-handle for the conductor to haul himself up for consultations with his driver.

Across the street the availability of Scotch Ales is advertised, but Eastern Counties No. LFS 100 (DAH 400B) promotes the local product, brewed not far away at Bury St Edmunds. One would like to think that the two bicycles – a nice Cambridge touch – belonged to undergraduates from Girton, and that their baskets were freighted with books about emission spectra in singly ionised atoms. The photograph was taken on Thursday 11 August 1977. Some forty years later I came to live not far away. On my occasional visits to Cambridge, narrowing my eyes to shut out the yellow lines, *Big Issue* sellers, wheelie-bins and surveillance cameras, the mirage of an FS sometimes appears, swinging out into the traffic from a side street far ahead.

Lincolnshire Road Car's No. 2342 (PBE 121) was seeing out its last years as a driver trainer, numbered DT1. Aspirant drivers stare back at the camera, each awaiting his next bout with the crash box, vacuum brakes and emphatically unassisted steering. If, after three days or so, he survives the 'prelim' – at which the examiner expects to see some evidence of aptitude – he faces his 'final' and, if successful, a PSV driver's licence and badge. The process of learning – not at all the same thing as passing a test – then begins.

Western SMT used this rather austere battleship grey for its training fleet, but retaining both cream bands, edged with black. The colour-scheme served to throw the splendid fleetname lettering into relief. In the background a roll-call of once familiar high street names: Woolworth's, Saxone, John Collier, Dunn and Abbey National have all gone; only H. Samuel and Boots are still with us. The bus, originally No. B1810 (VCS 364), was photographed in Paisley on Wednesday 17 May 1978.

'There's a high step, conductor.' Several times a day we heard this ritual complaint from the old dears. One conductor I knew was in the habit of reaching under the stairs ('Hang on Luv, I'll lower it for you') and pretending to adjust an invisible mechanism – the passenger invariably thanking him and agreeing that the step was now more easily negotiable. This is the only example I saw of one of these split-level platforms. But is the dropped step actually lower than a standard platform? It is flush with the bottom edge of the side panels, as in any rear-entrance Lodekka, yet the higher part is level with the lower deck floor. It's a bit like one of those M. C. Escher drawings you used to see reproduced as posters in Athena. The bus, an FS6G, had been new in 1962 to Brighton, Hove & District, but was now No. 3494 with Hants & Dorset. It is seen in Southampton on Saturday 23 October 1976.

A couple of interlopers from the main Eastern Scottish fleet have infiltrated the Baxter's garage at Airdrie in this shot, taken Saturday 7 May 1977. This marvellously gloomy establishment – called the Victoria garage, I think – closed not long afterwards and its activities moved to the Eastern Scottish garage not far away at Clarkston. It was probably the end of the separate Baxter's identity as well. The bus, numbered into the main fleet as AA892 (YWS 892), was, in any case, a standard Eastern Scottish FLF6G.

A few operators went in for fitting hubcaps to the rear axles of their FLFs. By the date of this photograph, Thursday 6 January 1977, Western National must have been the last operator to continue the practice. No. 2113 (EDV 525D), new in 1966, is seen in Exeter Street, Plymouth. It was later exported through the dealer British Double Deckers and is believed to survive as a mobile servery in Wisconsin.

When, in 1934, Bristol Omnibus Co. took over operation of Gloucester's local services, it was agreed that the vehicles should remain a distinct fleet carrying the Gloucester name and the city's coat of arms. On Saturday 17 November 1979 both features were a little faded on the side panels of No. G7269 (HAE 278D) and the original form of the NBC 'double N' logo tells us that it was some time since the bus had visited the paint shop. Balancing the mileages of the vehicles in the company's sub-fleets for accounting purposes was an interesting aspect of its operation. A fortnight after the photo, as part of these arrangements, G7269 found itself reallocated to see out its last days on the Bristol city services.

The purpose of a bus service is to move the citizenry efficiently and cheaply from place to place in vehicles that are the expression of civic dignity. Base commercial considerations have no place in such an undertaking. The 'all-over' advertisement, a lamentable development of the 1970s, was soon supplemented by the lesser disfigurement we see here, known as a 'broadside' advertisement. Central SMT's No. BE222 (CGM 722C) is seen in Clyde Street, Glasgow, on Monday 15 May 1978, shortly after crossing the eponymous river on its approach to Anderston Cross bus station.

For the Lodekka fancier, South Wales was rather slim pickings. Red & White was the only company that operated a substantial fleet, but its territory was partly in England and it had no front-entrance examples. This would have meant, I think, that the small number of FSFs inherited from United Welsh by South Wales Transport were the only front-entrance Lodekkas in the region. No. 952 (153 ACY) is seen in Swansea on Friday 31 December 1976.

G. W. Osborne & Son, of Tollesbury in Essex, was a famous name among independent operators. Its fleet had traditionally included a number of prototypes and former demonstrators. These two FLFs, both with Bristol engines and acquired from the local 'company' operator, Eastern National, represented a more conventional purchase. On the left Eastern National No. 2800 (BVX 676B) had come to Osborne's in 1978; the former No. 2876 (STW 764D) had joined the fleet in 1979. The pair is seen at Tollesbury on Saturday 29 March 1980.

United Counties No. 664 (CNV 664B), an FS6B of 1964, enters Luton's bus station on Saturday 20 May 1978 ahead of one of the company's dual-door Bristol REs. On short local services the lazy man tried to get away with displaying a route number only, to avoid the bother of changing the blind at each terminus. Neither bus in the photo displays a destination. The railway line in the background has now been revamped as a 'busway'. The FS was then in its final days and was withdrawn later in the year.

'Wouldn't pull the skin off a rice pudding,' was the driver's traditional complaint, with others unsuitable for reproduction in a publication intended for family reading. The FLF was somewhat underpowered with the Bristol BVW or Gardner LW engine, but some operators took advantage of the option to fit the Gardner LX, at 10.45 litres a considerable improvement. Central SMT's buying policy was rather inconsistent however: its early 'long' FLFs were provided with the LW; the later examples benefited from the LX, but had only four-speed gearboxes. Seating capacities varied according to the provision of additional luggage space. No. BL319 (FGM 319D) is seen leaving Glasgow on Saturday 7 May 1977 on the service to Hairmyres Hospital.

Eastern Scottish FLF No. AA982 (KPW 483E) gleams in the pre-breakfast sunshine of a Glasgow spring morning, Tuesday 16 May 1978, displaying to good advantage its dignified livery and discreetly underlined fleetname. The bus had been new in 1967 and come to Scotland from the Eastern Counties fleet in 1973. The oddly assorted windows were a feature of Eastern Scottish vehicles in Glasgow, where stoning buses was a popular pastime on some of the less favoured housing estates. After passing through the hands of several dealers and preservationists, the bus was acquired by the Bremen Airport Authority and was modified with an offside rear entrance and a slightly lowered roof.

Only forty-two of the 30-foot rear-entrance FLs were built, of which Red & White owned thirty. The company's No. L1660 (16 AAX) is pictured at Newport bus station on Friday 25 March 1977 alongside one of the town's Alexander-bodied Leyland Atlanteans. Note that these longer buses were required to provide an extra emergency exit in the lower deck bay behind the cab.

A shot from the forecourt of Eastern National's Wood Green garage, in north London, where many of the interior scenes from *On the Buses* were filmed. A Bob Grant-style wide boy wears uniform accessorised with platform shoes, non-issue trousers of approximately the correct shade, a mysterious wrist-band and satchel worn on the hip. The company's No. 2929 (AVW 398F), a 'long' semi-automatic FLF, is made ready for its next trip on the service to Southend. The 'Pay as You Enter' sign and modified cabside were souvenirs of a scheme, rejected by the men's union, to convert these vehicles to driver-only operation.

At Motherwell, deep in its heartland south-east of Glasgow, Central SMT, like neighbouring Eastern Scottish and Alexander Fife, was still operating considerable numbers of rear-entrance Lodekkas. B205 (AGM 705B), an FS dating from 1964, threads its way through reconstruction-impeded traffic on Wednesday 18 May 1978.

'Passengers! ...I dunno. They comes in the bus entrance, they roams around on the apron, and if you gets a bit too close to 'em, they looks at you as though iss yore fault!' Southern Vectis FLF No. 609 (CDL 477C) dodges a drifting party of amusement-hungry holidaymakers at Ryde Esplanade on Monday 15 August 1977. Following its withdrawal the bus was exported to the United States, where it subsequently donated its registration number and other marks of identification to an ex-Mansfield District example thought to survive in Washington State.

On Thursday 28 June 1979, Eastern Scottish No. AA217 (GSG 217D) waits to leave St Andrew Square bus station, Edinburgh, on the service to Birkenside – a housing estate just off the A7 south of the city. The driver, welcoming the opportunity to stretch his legs, stands alongside. Both he and the bus would have belonged to Eastern Scottish's Dalkeith garage, at the halfway point of the route.

From all over the country 'time-expired' buses converged upon Carlton, near Barnsley, usually for the grisly rites of the breaker's yard. A few survived for a further period of use, usually among fleets in the independent sector. The buses seen here, including the former Western SMT No. B1936 (XCS 957), look in reasonable nick and may have been set aside as 'goers'. The photograph was taken (shortly before the photographer was sent packing) at the premises of the dealer PVS on Tuesday 3 July 1979. Note the engaging little bus alongside, a Willowbrook-bodied Albion Nimbus from the fleet of Booth & Fisher of Halfway, near Sheffield. It would have spent most of its life on colliery contracts.

Where today palisade fencing and security cameras would be found, concrete posts and chicken wire suffice to separate Kensington depot, Bath, from the stud-impressed goalmouth of the neighbouring sports field. Gardner-engined FSF No. 6006 (703 JHY) awaits the afternoon's school buses and peak-hour extras on Monday 22 December 1975. It was a veteran of the Gloucester city fleet and was to be withdrawn some six months later in a wave of service 'revisions' – i.e. reductions.

Seen in Mansfield on Saturday 5 May 1979, this FS6G had entered service in 1961 as Midland General's No. 500 (915 MRB). Its subsequent history had partaken of the bewildering complexities of management and ownership in the region after the NBC takeover. It gravitated to East Midlands Motor Services in 1975, by way of Mansfield District Traction. The trainee prepares for his getaway from the lights. In training, first gear was insisted upon for hill starts, defined as 'any situation in which you feel the bus might roll backwards if you released the handbrake'.

A breakdown wagon obviously adapted from an LD Lodekka – and an early one too, judging by the 'droopy' front window and the curved bottom of the cabside windows – tows a stricken vehicle into Alexander Fife's Kirkcaldy garage on Tuesday 26 June 1979. The bus had started life in 1956 as No. FRD 8 (GWG 984) and been converted to a recovery lorry in 1972. In this condition it remained in use until 1981.

Eastern National No. 2813 (GNO 789B) must have been among the earliest recipients of the re-designed front lower deck window, introduced around the time it was new. This eliminated the little viewing tunnel between the cab and the inside of the bus, somewhat improving the driver's view of the platform. The bus is seen climbing North Hill, Colchester, on Tuesday 15 March 1977. In its wake follows an interesting procession of what would now be regarded as classic cars.

This is how we saw them: out of the corner of the eye, part of the surroundings, hardly noticed as we stepped between parked cars and glanced along the street before crossing. On Saturday 7 May 1977, Alexander Midland No. MRD 161 (TWG 531) swings out from one of Dunfermline's two bus stations. One hears again the snarl of the Gardner engine taken up to its top revs and the faint grunt of cog-teeth in the over-hasty uphill gearchange. The passengers' heads sway in unison as the driver releases his hold on the wheel and the bus comes out of its slight list. He cannily hangs back, in the expectation that the lights will change to green before he reaches them and, becoming gradually less audible, the bus accelerates into the distance.

Seen on one of Salisbury's local services on Friday 23 January 1976 was Hants & Dorset No. 108 (683 AAM). An FS6G, the bus had been new in 1962 to Wilts & Dorset, which must have specified the superior, non-standard seating. The two companies had been placed under common management in 1965 and were fully merged under NBC auspices in 1972. A compromise was struck whereby the H&D name was used, but the W&D red livery was retained. The bus is believed to survive in the Netherlands, super-powered by a Gardner LX engine.

In 1969, Bristol Omnibus Co. was prevailed upon to donate all but one of its Gardner-engined city-fleet FLFs to the West Riding Automobile Co. The latter had been closely involved in development of the innovative but catastrophically unsuccessful Guy Wulfrunian. West Riding bought almost all that were built and had been compelled to withdraw them after short service lives. Bristol was among several NBC companies that stepped in to provide replacements for the *avant-garde* Wolverhampton-made vehicles. It was the undoing of Guy Motors. The former Bristol No. C7227 (EHT 116C) is seen at Wakefield on Tuesday 16 October 1976.

York Place, Edinburgh, was the approach to the city's bus station and always provided a bumper yield of passing vehicles to the visiting lensman. On Tuesday 16 May 1978, Eastern Scottish 'long' FLF No. AA226 (GSG 226D) turns in with the destination display already 'dressed' for the next outward journey. The cowl looks slightly non-standard, lacking a foot-step.

On the first day of 1970 Western National's enclave at Trowbridge was transferred to Bristol Omnibus Co. Among the vehicles that changed hands were eight Bristol-engined FLFs, including No. 7315 (818 KDV), new in 1963 and seen in the town, noted for sausages, on Friday 23 January 1976. Their side-by-side destination screens and Exeter registrations always made the ex-Western National FLFs conspicuous among Bristol's own. This one was eventually exported to the United States and is thought to survive, re-equipped with American running units.

Still faithfully discharging its former owner's obligations under an advertising contract with the *Essex Chronicle*, a former Eastern National FLF stands half dismembered in one of the Carlton breakers' yards on Tuesday 3 July 1979. At the time I identified the vehicle from its chassis number but, alas, the information was lost when, some years later, I threw away a large number of photographs. Madness. I had recorded details on the reverse of each print. All the photographs in this book are reproduced from their negatives which, fortunately, I retained.

Central SMT's no BE236 (CGM 736C) stands at Anderston Cross, Glasgow, early on Wednesday 17 May 1978. An extra luggage rack, visible behind the first lower deck window, reduced seating capacity to sixty-eight. Central must have been the last major advocate of applying the relief colour to the window surrounds. Later, when the SBG corporate logo was introduced, the relief colour was extended upwards, to the level of the 'tween decks band, avoiding the awkward 'step down' behind the cab.

Fresh off the train from Carlisle, I arrived at Whitehaven on Friday 29 June 1979 to find the way into the town lined with buses, all nicely arranged in the open and easily photographed. It might have been laid on for me alone. The former railway land in front of the station had been annexed by the neighbouring Cumberland Motor Services garage. Gardner LX-engined No. 519 (713 GRM) was looking a little worn at the edges, as it had a right to after giving faithfully of its services for seventeen years. The land is now the car park of a Tesco store.

Well, it's not the way I was taught. The approved method of dismounting from the vehicle was backwards, lowering one's self to the ground holding onto a grab-handle and using the foot step. This was an undignified proceeding, which brought the hindquarters into unwelcome prominence. The true bus driver used the 'flying leap' method captured in the photograph. This was not without its dangers and a driver I knew was taken to hospital after landing on the bonnet of a passing Cortina. This vehicle entered service as Crosville's No. DFB 96 (906 VFM) in February 1962. It is seen in Liverpool on Monday 16 February 1976. On CBC-fitted Lodekkas the radiator grille was a dummy and an early photograph of the bus shows it running with a 'blank' front cowl. These appeared in several fleets but were not considered an aesthetic success.

Not, technically, the greatest of photos, but not the greatest day for taking it. Not able to stand back far enough to 'get it all in', I was forced to employ a wide-angle lens whose quality fell some way short of superb. Nonetheless, the photograph has always been a favourite of mine, partly because it shows one of the great bus liveries, but also because Glasgow on a day of autumn drizzle, as the light began to fail during the afternoon was, to me, Glasgow at its most beautiful. The picture dates from Monday 18 October 1976 and was taken in the soon-to-disappear Dundas Street bus station. Alexander Midland's No. MRD 184 (VWG 364), allocated to Kirkintilloch garage, was new in 1963.

United was early in getting rid of its Lodekkas. The Gardner-engined FLFs had gone to Scotland and the Bristol BVW engine with CBC system was not always a happy combination. Bristol engine spares were also becoming difficult to obtain. United's last FLFs disappeared during 1979. On Wednesday 20 October 1976, this early example must have been living on borrowed time. No. 394 (5094 HN), from the second FLF sanction, had been new in February 1962. It is seen at Newcastle's Haymarket bus station squeezing between an inconsiderately parked Ford Escort 1300 and an early Bristol RE in its final month of service.

Eastern Scottish No. AA887 (YWS 887), a 1962 FLF, seen at Airdrie's bus station on Saturday 7 May 1977. I travelled up from Bristol by sleeper (never again!) and returned by the same means that evening. Rather than the balmy spring day and good light I had hoped for, chilly gusts from the Firth of Clyde herded rain-burdened clouds across this bleak periphery of the Glasgow suburbs. Illuminated offside advertisement panels came and went on the sides of Lodekkas according to no identifiable pattern. The bus went on to become a training vehicle, painted in an eye-catching yellow and blue colour-scheme.

United Counties was somehow one of the Cinderellas of the NBC, a little-known subsidiary serving anonymous places such as Dunstable and Biggleswade. As a connoisseur of dullness, I always had a soft spot for it. On Saturday 20 May 1978, in Church Street, Luton, No. 670 (CNV 670B), a Bristol-engined FS dating from 1964, looks none the better for the dermatitis of scruffy paper notices in its lower deck windows. These, usually giving notification of fare increases, were a semi-permanent feature during the seventies.

Following its withdrawal, Bristol loaned its No. 7050 (218 NAE) to Crosville Motor Services for several months. Upon its return the bus was acquired by Dann Catering as a 'location kitchen'. It was repainted in the Bristol Omnibus Co. paint shop. There was nothing for it but to fork out the 50p admission fee to get this photograph of the vehicle at the annual Bristol Flower Show. It was Friday 1 September 1978.

Still fitted with the sixty-five coach seats with which it had entered service in 1964, Alder Valley's No. 637 (ABL 117B) reposes in the yard of the company's Reading garage on Monday 29 March 1976. The vehicle had been Thames Valley's No. D5 and was a veteran of the limited stop service from Reading to London.

Alexander Northern had bought no Lodekkas new, but in 1978 became the third owner of six FLFs that had originated with Eastern National and come to Scotland in exchange for Alexander Midland VRTs. Thus the FLF appeared in yet another of the Scottish Bus Group's multifarious liveries – this one, perhaps, more remarkable for its unorthodoxy than its beauty. No. NRD 3 (RVW 394D) was photographed at Seagate bus station, Dundee, on Tuesday 26 June 1979.

A look at the lower deck interior of an FLF. Bristol Omnibus Co. No. 7014 (809 MHW) was among the first of those with moquette upholstery and florescent lighting, a great improvement on the tungsten bulbs and dark green leather (not vinyl) of its immediate predecessors. The inward-facing seats, never popular with passengers, were raised to clear the wheel arches, suspension and drop-centre axle. The conductor's customary post at the foot of the stairs was more convenient than in the LD and FS and nicely set back from the platform and gangway. This pair of shots was taken on Monday 28 April 1975.

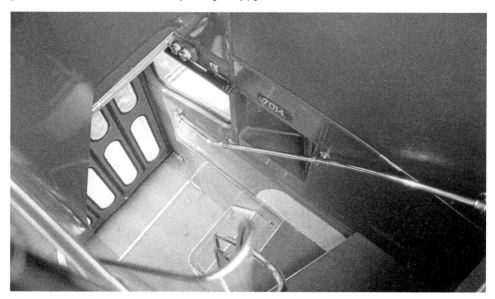

Getting into the detail. A view down the stairs to the platform of Bristol's No. 7014. Beneath the fleet number plate is the viewing tunnel from the cab, eliminated in a later re-design. The two switches turned on the lights for the cleaners who swept out the interiors by night. Their least enviable task was to attend to 'vomit jobs'. The bottom two steps were hinged and could be lifted for access to the clutch and gearbox. They were not fixed, but merely held in place by gravity, which meant that there was always a little free movement. As a young conductor I learned that I could slide from close to the top of the stairs using the stanchions as 'guide rails' and landing with a tremendous bang on the bottom step. This was an excellent means of getting the lower deck passengers to pay attention and start getting their fares ready. Tricks of the trade; it all came with experience.

Another of Western SMT's ex Alder Valley FLFs with the original 'T-box' masked by an inverted SBG destination screen. Examples of that typical and ubiquitous Scottish bus, the Alexander-bodied Leyland Leopard, crowd around No. B2440 (PBL 59F) on Monday 25 June 1979. My train from Bristol had arrived in Glasgow at around 1.30 p.m. It was the start of a five-day bus-snapping holiday. I'd booked into the hotel and was already out here at Paisley by 3.10. Pretty good footwork.

I had seen this bus from the window of a train on the way back from Brighton. Seconds later we passed through a station, enabling me to get a 'fix'. The station, since closed, was Coulsdon North. The bus, in what I remember as a pleasing blue and grey livery, looked to be in an easily photographed position. It had been a Saturday. The thought rankled and, the following Wednesday, 4 July 1979, I returned. Contrary to my earlier impression, the bus was not at all easy to photograph; this was about the best I could manage. It proved to be the former Western National No. 2089 (BOD 31C), withdrawn in April 1978 and acquired by the Purley Car Co. Ltd of Warlingham, trading as Hardy's Coaches. Already it was derelict and is reported scrapped in June 1980.

Apart from when it is brand new, no bus looks as good as when it has just come out of the works. Now twelve years old, Bristol's No. C7285 (JAE 94D) had probably just had its second recertification overhaul. The company had re-engined many of its newest Bristol-engined FLFs with Gardner LWs, to ensure a supply of spares into their old age. Reeking of fresh paint, the vehicle is seen at the Central Repair Works, Lawrence Hill, on Thursday 23 March 1978. The LW was an aesthetically pleasing engine and its appearance was not improved by the company's practice of spraying the entire inside of the engine compartment with a coating of protective silver paint.

Carrying a respectable load Eastern Scottish No. AA884 (YWS 884), an FLF dating from 1962 and a veteran of the Baxter's fleet, turns into North Hanover Street, Glasgow, on Monday 25 June 1979, shortly after leaving the Buchanan bus station. It is fitted with one of the company's peculiar home-made radiator grilles.

Eastern National's No. 2900 (WVX 527F) was a 31-foot FLF with semi-automatic transmission, Gardner LX engine, forward-ascending staircase and additional luggage accommodation, which kept the seating capacity down to seventy. A friend and I, seeking permission to enter the garage's parking area and identifying ourselves as NBC staff from Bristol, were received by the garage's manager as visiting dignitaries. We were bidden to the staff canteen. We accepted this well-meant offer more from good manners than because we were in need of refreshment and ascended a flight of narrow stairs. At the next table money changed hands between a driver who had some pressing need to avoid working his final journey and a colleague who was willing to 'cover' it for him. Thirteen years later, when it was owned by Top Deck Travel, I encountered the bus again in Paris.

Hants & Dorset No. 1113 (5675 EL), a Gardner-engined FS dating from 1960, seen at Fareham bus station on Monday 15 August 1977. It went on to serve as a driver trainer with both Western National and Devon General and survives in preservation. The lower-case letters used by Hants & Dorset for its destination blinds were supposed to be – and probably were – more legible from a distance, but I'm rather glad the idea was not taken up by other operators.

The weather was doing its best to supply the rainy, cloud-dimmed poetry of Glasgow, but the new Buchanan bus station and its prosaic redeveloped surroundings neutralised the effect, leaving only squalor. Alexander Midland's No. MRD 181 (VWG 361), dating from 1963, sloshes through the puddles to reach its 'stance' at the platform. It was all in the detail, and this beautiful livery would not have looked nearly so good without the black wings and black lining-out of the cream bands.

A 1956 LD, originally No. MG790 (XFM 201) but, from 1958, when Crosville changed its fleet numbering system, renumbered as DLG790. For its second career as a training vehicle the first two letters had been painted out. The photograph was taken on Monday 16 February 1976 in Moorfields, Liverpool. At the top of the street we catch a glimpse of Exchange station, which was to close the following year. Its services passed to the new Moorfields station, off right of this view.

Still carrying its 'dustbin lid' rear hubcaps, Western National's FLF No. 2102 (EDV 514D) is seen in Taunton on Thursday 19 February 1976. Across the street is one of the former Bristol Omnibus Co. FSFs, acquired in 1967.

'Dressed' for Hairmyres Hospitial (*sic*), a Central SMT long FLF poses in the evening sunshine at the periphery of Glasgow's Buchanan bus station where, although the facilities had been in use for over a year, construction appears to be incomplete. BL278 (EGM 278C) was a seventy-eight-seater new in 1965. Alongside, and far from home, is a Plaxton-bodied AEC Reliance belonging to Armchair Coaches of Brentford. The photograph was taken on Tuesday 16 May 1978.

Bristol's No. 6024 (726 JHY), a 1961 FSF, had been one of those passed to Western National in 1967 when that company had required twenty of the type at a time when it was no longer available. Shortly before the 1970 transfer of its Trowbridge operation to Bristol Omnibus Co., the fickle Western National company slyly re-allocated several ancient or unwanted buses to Trowbridge so that they would pass to the Bristol company. They included several FSFs, which thus 'came home' to see out their final years with their original owner. No. 6024 is seen in Bath on Thursday 16 October 1975 during this second phase of its Bristol career.

1962 Eastern Scottish FLF No. AA893 (YWS 893), photographed at the company's Bathgate garage on Thursday 28 June 1979. Alongside is one of the many splendid ex-military AEC Matador gun tractors that found further employment as breakdown wagons in the auxiliary fleets of bus operators.

Chugging past the Scunthorpe Co-op on Monday 9 October 1978 was Lincolnshire Road Car No.2533 (CVL 410D), a five-cylinder FS dating from 1966. The winter that followed was severe and this was one of three FS5Gs that Lincolnshire loaned to West Yorkshire Road Car to cover for more modern vehicles that had not stood up so well to the weather. When spring came, the FSs were withdrawn.

We remain in the flat easterly extremities of England where, on Saturday 20 May 1978, we encounter another FS5G, this time in the Eastern Counties fleet. As can be seen, Lodekkas were being ousted from the Cambridge city services by Bristol VRTs, the one on the left having come from Western SMT in exchange for an FLF. The Premier Travel Plaxton-bodied AEC Reliance appears to be operating a tour of Cambridge. No. LFS73 (AAH 173B) still had two and a half years of service ahead of it.

In a street lined with useful shops where today financial services and kebab takeaways are found, we see Crosville's No. DFG 76 (886 VFM), a 1962 FSF. The photo was taken in Crewe on Monday 16 February 1976, on the walk from the station to the bus station. The locution 'train station' is not used by careful native-born speakers of English (Americans may be excused) and should be ridiculed whenever encountered. The product advertised on the side of the bus, popularly 'Worthy', was then still a household name.

Down on the Isle of Wight, Southern Vectis continued to get faithful service from its ageing fleet of LDs. No. 555 (ODL 15), with open platform bodywork, was approaching its twentieth birthday when seen leaving Newport bus station on Monday 15 August 1977. For the mid-morning lull the bus carries a respectable load, probably augmented at this time of year by holidaymakers. Following its withdrawal the bus is believed to have been exported, but in 2012 turned up outside the Design Centre in Islington as the centrepiece of an eye-catching example of 'installation art'.

The former Western National No. 1967 (519 BTA), seen during its later career as a training vehicle. Being allocated to Taunton, it had wandered a little from its usual haunts and was photographed in the shadow of one of the mighty bonded warehouses serving Bristol's tobacco industry ...this one felled by explosives in 1988. The bus is believed to survive and to be in store pending restoration. If this bus is compared with the LD in the previous photograph, it will be seen that ECW tidied up the window spacing in this, the FS, and eliminated the untidy small window next to the platform.

Sliding vents alternate with hoppers both upstairs and down on Alexander Midland's No. MRD 208 (UEV 220E), which had come from the Eastern National fleet in 1971. It is seen parked in Glasgow's evening sunshine awaiting departure on a peak hours only service to Campsie Glen. By Thursday 28 June 1979, the beauty of the company's livery had been compromised by the Scottish Bus Group's new corporate fleetname.

The trainee gets his lock on and swings around in the road outside Cumberland Motor Services' bus station (left) and garage (right) at Whitehaven on Friday 29 June 1979. The bus had been No. 554 (113 DRM) in its revenue-earning days. As part of the internal modifications for its training role, the fuel tank was moved, which accounts for the odd position of the filler cap. Upstairs we can just make out a projector screen for slide shows.

Eastern Scottish AA995 (RHN 948F) has enjoyed a long and varied career. It had been new in 1968 and came to Scotland from United Automobile Services. Eastern Scottish placed it with its Baxter's subsidiary, but by the time of the photograph, taken in Leith Street, Edinburgh, on Tuesday 16 May 1978, it had become part of the main fleet. Following its withdrawal the bus was used as a driver trainer by Alexander Midland, but was then exported and passed through the hands of various owners in Germany and the Netherlands, where it is thought to survive.

The former Bristol Omnibus Co. No. C6010 (709 JHY), still carrying its C (for 'city') prefix Bristol Joint Services fleet number, is seen turning into Bridge Street, Salisbury, on Monday 22 May 1978. The Bristol-engined FSF had been taken out of service at the end of June 1976, among the first batch of forward-entrance buses withdrawn by the company. It passed to the well-known Barnsley dealer Paul Sykes and thence to Odstock Hospital, just outside Salisbury, for staff transport. It was heading for Salisbury General Hospital, a few yards behind the camera. Note the inevitable 999 'route number'.

The humble No. 78 Brightlingsea to Colchester North Station service seems lowly work for this semi-automatic, LX-powered 31-footer. Eastern National's No. 2913 (WWC 743F), not yet ten years old, had already been 'cascaded' from more prestigious duties. The conductor, clutching his machine case, hurries to consult with his driver before departure. Following withdrawal this was one of many Lodekkas that found their way into the fleet of Top Deck Travel. It was exported to the Netherlands in 1997 and re-registered locally. It has passed through the hands of several owners and is thought to be still active.

In town and country, parked at lonely lay-bys far beyond the houses, disgorging shoppers onto thronged high streets, depositing holidaymakers on blowy esplanades, on the fells and in the dales, the rear-entrance double-decker yet retained a precarious hold on the public transport scene at the beginning of the eighties. As far as the Lodekka was concerned, the survivors were mostly of the FS type. As the new decade opens, United Counties No. 682 (EBD 682C), a Bristol-engined example dating from 1965, is seen in Northampton on Thursday 17 January 1980. The driver retains his hold on the clockwork indicator switch to prevent it from self-cancelling as he waits to join the traffic.

A couple of weeks in arrears of southern England, the trees burst into leaf as spring arrives in Kirkcaldy. On Tuesday 16 May 1978, Alexander Fife No. FRD 188 (BXA 453B) basks in the welcome sunshine as Morag, late back to the office from her lunch hour, puts her best sensibly-shod foot forward. Or was she merely dashing to catch that Daimler Fleetline in the background?

Seen passing the East Midland Motor Services garage in Mansfield on Tuesday 16 August 1977 is Mansfield District Traction No. 451 (DAL 306C), a Gardner-engined FLF of 1965. In this rare example of a Mansfield vehicle carrying an advertisement, an 'in-house' product is promoted.

Brake cooling was not the only problem associated with the deeper front wings introduced in 1962: minor accidents sometimes resulted from the angled corners making contact with other vehicles during manoeuvres in traffic. The 'rounding-off' we see here was one remedy. Many operators simply cut the wings back to a level just below the headlights. United's No. 447 (147 SHN), a Bristol-engined FLF of 1964, is seen in Newcastle on Wednesday 20 October 1976. The Alexander-bodied Daimler Fleetline belonged to NBC subsidiary Northern General.

The sub-fleets within the Bristol Omnibus Co. were a fascinating study to the enthusiast. The 388 was one of the 'Hanham Local Services', inherited in 1936 from an independent operator, that served suburbs beyond Bristol's boundary in south Gloucestershire. Accordingly they could not be incorporated into the 'city' services. All these interesting anomalies would soon be at an end, for the joint agreement between the company and the city council had ended during 1978, and the Bristol fleet became a single entity. Gardner-engined No. 7170 (BHU 19C), lately transferred from the Gloucester city fleet, is seen battling through the snow at Cadbury Heath on Thursday 15 February 1979.

An ex-Wilts & Dorset vehicle (no sun visor) in the Hants & Dorset fleet, seen in Salisbury on Saturday 23 October 1976. The two operators were merged by the National Bus Company in 1972. In the 1980s the Wilts & Dorset name was revived as the NBC's subsidiaries were broken up into smaller units for sale into private hands. This bus became one of the restored company's training vehicles. No. 215 (EMR 296D) had entered service in November 1966.

In Scotland late examples of the LD-type, such as Eastern Scottish No. AA855 (WSC 855), seen here in Glasgow on Monday 25 June 1979, soldiered on into the eighties. The slotted panels covering the CBC openings on either side of the destination box were a characteristic feature of Eastern Scottish Lodekkas and somewhat tidied the appearance of the vehicle. They were, I think, inverted duplicates of the vents used at the side.

Considering that they are so often found masquerading abroad as 'London buses', it is ironic that Lodekkas were actually a rare sight in the capital. In their latter years they appeared in the metropolis only on Eastern National's services from Wood Green. Photographed from the central reservation of a dual-carriageway in Romford, No. 2905 (WVX 532F), from Brentwood garage, is seen in the company of several London Transport vehicles. A Routemaster passes on the 175 service, but the other buses have a look of the NBC about them. One was conscious of a homogenising process at work. The FLF survived into the post-deregulation era and went on to serve Stagecoach in Scotland. It was scrapped in 1988.

The front seat upper deck passenger takes a drag on her cigarette, as one still could in that less regulated age, as Crosville's No. DFG 72 (882 VFM), a 1962 FSF6G, awaits departure from Crewe bus station on Monday 16 February 1976. In 1979 the bus was converted for use as an open-topper at Rhyl. It subsequently enjoyed a long career in promotional work for a firm of estate agents and is thought to survive in preservation.

United Counties operated comparatively few FLFs. Smallish batches entered service among larger numbers of the FS, which the company continued to take into stock for as long as it remained available. Being Bristol-engined, not many of the FLFs survived to an advanced age. Seen in Luton on Saturday 20 May 1978, No. 737 (LRP 737E), new in 1967, was withdrawn in September 1980 and scrapped.

Central SMT's No. BE270 (CGM 970C), photographed in Glasgow on Thursday 28 June 1979. The evening sunshine displays to advantage the company's handsome livery. The eye somehow demands that the cream band be continued along the sides, but this would have involved placing the fleetname lettering against a non-contrasting light background. I would guess that the rather awkward treatment seen here was devised around the avoidance of this undesirable effect. The bus is believed to have been ordered by Alexander Fife, which accounts for a number of departures from Central SMT's standard spec.

A smartly turned-out FS5G of Lincolnshire Road Car Co. seen passing Lincoln's bus station on Friday 12 August 1977. No. 2380 (OVL 475) had been new in 1961. Inwardly one hears again the distinctive and once very familiar five-cylinder Gardner acoustics.

Turning across the traffic into Hills Road garage, Cambridge, on Thursday 11 August 1977 is Eastern Counties No. FLF 465 (KAH 465D), dating from 1966. It was withdrawn in November 1984 and cannibalised for spares to keep another FLF in service. The garage survived the bus by less than a year and its site was rapidly redeveloped.

Displaying its discreet YORK WEST YORKSHIRE fleetname, West Yorkshire Road Car's No. 3798 (JWR 412C) passes an impressive formation of bus shelters, with large, informative bus stop flags. It was long before the coming of Adshel shelters. A faint rust-tinged streak beneath the coolant filler cap suggests recent 'boiling' problems. Careless fuelling has also not improved the vehicle's appearance. The Bristol-engined FS had been placed in traffic in December 1965 and is seen here beneath York's city wall on Wednesday 20 October 1976.

The former Thames Valley No. D30, now Alder Valley No. 662 (GRX 130D), makes its 'round the houses' approach to Reading's vile basement bus station where, high overhead in an exhaust-fogged void, diseased pigeons copulated on concrete ledges, among stalactites and blotches of limey efflorescence. Such facilities proliferated throughout Britain during the seventies. The bus had first entered revenue-earning service at the beginning of 1966 and is seen here on Monday 29 March 1976.

Western SMT's No. B2418 (SHN 254F) had been new in 1968 to United Automobile Co. and had then passed to its Tynemouth & District subsidiary. Curiouser and curiouser grew the adaptations of the CBC system: early photographs show the bus with vents on either side of the destination screen, but here they are absent. Presumably the equipment had been removed or isolated, which must have entailed the fitting of a conventional radiator. The bus is seen waiting for the traffic lights as it leaves Anderston Cross, Glasgow, on Wednesday 17 May 1978. This was another vehicle that later joined Top Deck Travel's fleet. In 1996 it was exported to the Netherlands, where it suffered the indignity of having its roof lowered to an overall height of 4m. It was finally destroyed by fire in 2010. Modern reflective number plates didn't suit the FLF.

Descending to the street from Chelmsford's rooftop station, I immediately recognised this bridge. A year or so before, as a trainee driver, I had been shown a video (I had been faintly surprised by the company's ownership of this up-to-the-minute item of equipment) explaining certain of the finer points of roadcraft. This location had been used in a sequence demonstrating the correct method of negotiating an arched bridge. The driver of Eastern National's No. 2854 (OVX 298D) – making a second appearance in this book – demonstrates the correct procedure on one of the 'town' services on Tuesday 15 March 1977.

Let us end with what is chronologically the last of these photographs, and one of the final photos I took of a bus. I think it was largely the disappearance of half-cabs like this and their succession by box-on-wheels, rear-engined, front-entrance buses suitable for driver-only operation that finally killed my interest in the subject. That, and unwelcome changes to the industry, in which I still worked. This ex-Red & White FL, now numbered T6 (13 AAX) in the training fleet of National Welsh (an NBC merger of the Red & White and Western Welsh companies), was pictured in Westgate Street, Cardiff, on Tuesday 13 December 1980. It looks as though the trainees are returning to their bus after a restorative cuppa at the bus station across the road. A delivery of gaseous, pressurised keg bitter arrives by lorry for the public house on the corner. Cheers!